AF407505

In memory of my beautiful Mr. Duke.

I hope this book will help dog parents understand the love, emotions and all that is involved with these amazing angels. But, in reality, I'm speaking on behalf of all animals on Earth.

I dedicate this book to my beautiful daughters Melissa and Gabrielle, who also learned to love and respect animals.

Thank you both for giving me two amazing dogs.

About the Author

Jenny Molina is a certified health coach in holistic nutrition. She believes the body can heal itself with proper nutrition and daily exercise. Jenny is now taking her approach to healing to the care of dogs after seeing how a healthy diet, combined with holistic supplements and daily therapy and walks extended the life of her dear Mr. Duke.

Contents

Arrival

August 2010 marked the beginning of an eventful day that would change the course of my life. As the morning sun peeked through the curtains, I savored my usual latte, followed by a strong black coffee. It was a typical day of phone calls and appointments. By evening's end I was exhausted.

Just as I had fallen asleep, a knock at the door shattered the tranquility of the night. Stirred from my slumber, I turned to my husband, questioning the late hour visitor. Who could it be? It was close to midnight. With a sense of intrigue, he opened the door and uttered the words that caught me off guard—"it'sMelissa".

With his endearing face, long ears, and droopy eyes, he exuded an undeniable charm. In that instant, my heart surrendered to this adorable canine, Mr. Duke, forever captivating my affections

Melissa? But she was in college in California. Why hadn't she called to let me know she was coming home?

Driven by a surge of curiosity and anticipation, I hurriedly made my way to the living room. And there she stood, her voice tender and her eyes, those beautiful hazel orbs radiating joy. In that moment, I knew something extraordinary awaited me. Perhaps she had a surprise to share, a secret she had kept hidden. And as I gazed upon the stroller beside her, my heart leaped with anticipation. Had she brought her bundle of joy into the world?

ut what I discovered beneath the blanket in stroller was not a human baby, as I had imagined, but a creature of a different kind — a puppy. With his endearing face, long ears, and droopy eyes, he exuded an undeniable charm. In that instant, my heart surrendered to this adorable canine, Mr. Duke, forever captivating my affections.

y daughter soon returned to California with Mr. Duke in tow, continuing her studies and embarking on adventures that would shape their bond. For two years, Mr. Duke lived a happy life, reveling in hunting excursions, and frolicking in the snowy landscapes of winter. It was a charmed existence, sharing love and companionship with my daughter and her boyfriend.

Separation

My daughter and Mr. Duke

But fate can be a fickle force, and one day, Mr. Duke's world was shattered. Like a child caught in the turbulence of parental separation, he lost the familiar comforts of favorite toys and the warmth of cuddles with mom and dad. No longer could he partake in the winter hunts with his beloved companion. My daughter returned to Miami, bearing the weight of sorrow and devastation. As I visited her, my heart ached at the palpable sadness in Mr. Duke's eyes. This was not the playful, exuberant puppy I had once known. He, too, had been consumed by sadness.

Mr. Duke looked at me with a gaze that transcended words, conveying a message that tugged at my heart. It was as if he beseeched me to care for him until his mother could navigate her own journey.

Reunion

Scooby

In my household resided another magnificent companion, Scooby, a brilliant Jack Russell terrier who had been my steadfast travel partner. Regretfully, my condo imposed a weight limit of 30 pounds, and Mr. Duke, a large American Foxhound now weighing over 75 pounds, exceeded this restriction.

After much pleading to the condo board, and by no small miracle, Mr. Duke was allowed to stay.

In the enchanting presence of Mr. Duke's radiant smile, a revelation washed over him, a realization that safety had embraced his being once again. Tears, brimming with an overflow of emotion, streamed down my face, bearing witness to the overwhelming joy that swelled within our hearts.

Unfathomable it seemed, the return of his presence, our beloved companion. Such resilience he possessed, an unwavering belief that we would come, that we would rescue him from the clutches of fate.

Since that remarkable day, Mr. Duke, merely a tender two years old, remained forever in our vigilant gaze.

Yet, destiny, relentless and capricious, conspired against us one fateful day as my husband embarked on a walk through the neighborhood, accompanied by both my cherished Scooby and the indomitable Mr. Duke.

While I prepared myself for the day's endeavors, a sudden ring of the telephone shattered the tranquility. My husband's voice, strained and frenzied, pierced through the receiver, recounting the heart-wrenching tale of Mr. Duke's loss.

A nightmare, it appeared, had taken hold of my reality.

An nightmare, it appeared
had taken hold…

Upon his return, my husband revealed the dreadful details—how they had found themselves at the intersection of a nearby block, when a driver lost control of the wheel and careened recklessly toward them. Instinct propelled my husband into swift action, shielding our tiny Scooby from the impending danger. Mr. Duke, gripped by terror, bolted with such force that broke his leash. My husband, straining to keep pace, pursued him, Scooby in his arms, as Mr. Duke vanished into the maelstrom of traffic. Anguish overwhelmed me, and in the depths of despair, I vowed not to relinquish my pursuit of him. I would not allow him to slip from our grasp.

Uncontrollable sobs rendered me incoherent, choking on my own tears. Hours turned into a whirlwind of ceaseless searching, a symphony of anguished pleas echoing within my mind — I could hear Mr. Duke calling to me, saying: "Keep searching for me, Grandma."

Surrender was not an option, for I knew deep within me that I could not abandon him.

Mr. Duke vanished into the maelstrom of traffic…

As hours passed, casting a shroud of despair over our weary hearts, a neighbor approached, bearing a glimmer of hope. She told us of two women opening a car door and Mr. Duke jumping eagerly into their vehicle. The location they described was just beyond the threshold of our building. The pieces aligned seamlessly, for Mr. Duke possessed an uncanny ability to find his way home, and the black vehicle she spoke of bore a striking resemblance to my own. In his confusion, Mr. Duke had mistaken it for my car, driven by an insatiable longing to reunite with his family.

Exhausted from our search, we returned home after five long hours.

Determined to leave no stone unturned, my husband and I embarked on a mission to disseminate flyers throughout the neighborhood, calling on both passersby and veterinary clinics within a ten-mile radius to aid in our quest. Exhausted from our search, we returned home after five long hours. Amidst our collective weariness, my husband, the weight of despair etched upon his face, whispered with a tremor in his voice, "I am sorry, it will be a challenge to find him, for such a beautiful dog will surely capture the heart of whoever discovers him. But we can't stop searching for him."

Hours of relentless pursuit had elapsed before my husband and I resolved to visit every nearby veterinarian, imploring them for any tidings of Mr. Duke's whereabouts. After several fruitless attempts, a flicker of hope materialized. News arrived that a man, had seen a dog fleeing amidst the tumult of a bustling thoroughfare and had rescued him. The description was that of our beloved Mr. Duke, a revelation that ignited hope within our hearts. The receptionist at the last clinic we visited, having seen the flyers that we had distributed earlier that day, recognized our dear Mr. Duke as the dog picked up by the gentleman. A deluge of disbelief swept over me, a torrent of emotion, after hours upon hours of desperate searching, praying for a miracle.

With trembling hands, I called the number provided by the benevolent stranger who had discovered Mr. Duke.

And at that moment, I knew that I would be reunited with my cherished Mr. Duke.

  With trembling hands, I called the
number provided by the benevolent
stranger who had discovered Mr.
Duke and arranged to meet outside
the veterinary clinic. Fifty minutes,
which seemed like an eternity, passed
before he arrived, hurriedly walking
Mr. Duke with an improvised rope
leash . Across the threshold of my
vision, I beheld a wondrous sight — a
convergence of Mr. Duke's enchanting
almond-shaped eyes, his resplendent
floppy ears, and the boundless joy that
radiated from his very being. Time
halted as if suspended in the ethereal
tapestry of existence. It was indeed
Mr. Duke.

Tears of joy streamed down my face as a wave of happiness and relief overtook me. Mr. Duke, filled with exuberance and excitement, jumped towards me with a symphony of smiles and leaps. It was a blissful moment, and I felt my soul mirror the same euphoria as his ecstatic dance.

From that moment onward, our connection blossomed, intertwining our lives with an unbreakable bond. I recognized the yearning within Mr. Duke's spirit, a longing for a resplendent realm far removed from the clamor of concrete and ceaseless traffic.

Contemplation swirled within my thoughts, as I toyed with the idea of seeking solace in a land adorned with verdant pathways, where he could thrive amidst nature's embrace. And so it came to pass that by the end of 2016, my husband and I embarked upon a pilgrimage, our hearts alight with anticipation, toward North Carolina. Its enchantment enveloped us, basking in the caress of perfect weather and the embrace of abundant greenways, a utopia for our dear Mr. Duke.

I toyed with the idea of seeking solace in a land adorned with verdant pathways

New Land

I could already perceive the flames of curiosity flickering within his eyes, beckoning him to explore this bountiful tapestry.

We both enjoyed our quiet walks in the trails, with our solitude only broken by the melodic chirping of birds, the gentle hum of crickets, the rustling of squirrels and the occasional hiker or a family of deer that crossed our path.

It was during these long walks that I would talk and softly sing to Mr. Duke, and he would look at me and smile, as if saying, "...I understand".

I knew he was glad we had left the city and all the noise and pollution for this paradise.

Such was his charm,
his magnetism

Together, we embarked on countless journeys, traversing landscapes both familiar and foreign, all the while weaving an indelible thread within the fabric of our neighborhood. Mr. Duke, a name on every tongue, etched his presence into the hearts of all who encountered him.

He quickly learned all of the places where treats would be freely available and clean, cool water could be had– the hardware store, the pet shop, the fishing supply, the local jeweler, and even the upscale clothier.

Such was his charm, his magnetism, an enchantment that bestowed upon me the privilege of experiencing a multitude of emotions thanks to his unwavering companionship.

He became my confidant, a companion who possessed an innate understanding of my mood, and every state of mind. I favored those times when we took long walks as they helped me to be in control of the anxieties and panic attacks I'd suffered since childhood. His presence was both soothing and comforting.

Failing Health

As the seasons unfolded, I perceived a shift in his essence—a weariness that manifested in the cadence of his steps, a lethargy that dulled his spirit. An ardent determination emerged within me, compelling me to take my beloved Mr. Duke to the veterinarian. After all, he had matured into a magnificent American Foxhound, nearing the pinnacle of his prime.

Apprehension mixed with love as I witnessed failing mobility, his once graceful gait reduced to a languid shuffle. That morning, as we embarked upon our solemn trip to the clinic, he no longer walked great distances.

My husband, bearing the weight
of determination upon his
shoulders, tenderly helped Mr.
Duke to our SUV. My heart
trembled, teetering
on the precipice of despair. His
cessation of movement had come
with an inexplicable suddenness,
robbing my beloved Mr. Duke of his
vitality.

Her countenance bore
an unspoken truth…

Upon arriving at the veterinary, I prayed, hoping for a miracle, for a revelation that would cast aside uncertainty.

The halls resonated with hushed whispers, a symphony of somber apprehension, until finally, the veterinarian emerged. Her countenance bore an unspoken truth, a truth I feared to hear.

In a voice tinged with melancholy, she spoke of Mr. Duke's advanced age, thirteen, the inevitability of ailments befalling noble creatures such as he. Arthritis, had gripped him with tenacious claws, its hold unrelenting. She uttered words that pierced my soul, words of a final farewell, a decision to be made, a decision I was not prepared to face. My husband and I united in our despair, left, tears on our faces, for we could not bear the thought of losing our beloved Mr. Duke.

I, however, refused to succumb to the inevitable. And so, we embarked on a journey of hope, of unyielding persistence, delving into the realms of alternative medicine, seeking solace within the embrace of holistic healing.

I, however, refused to
succumb to
the inevitable.

We subjected him to numerous sessions, witnessing incremental improvements...

Cold Laser Therapy emerged as a beacon of promise, its radiant light illuminating a path toward potential respite for Mr. Duke's weary joints. We subjected him to numerous sessions, witnessing incremental improvements that seeped into the crevices of our longing hearts.
But daily travel to a distant clinic weighed heavily upon us. In our unwavering devotion, we bought a device that would bring therapy into the warmth of our own home.

Before Cold Laser Therapy, he'd slowed down, his movements were lethargic and he'd spend more time laying down not walking as before...

Even in his final days, and after intensive therapy, Mr. Duke enjoyed his walks, much slower now, in the trails and greenways of North Carolina. One could see it in his gentle and grateful smile.

Nutrition & Healing

My husband remained steadfast, devoting thirty minutes each morning and evening to the well-being of our beloved Mr. Duke. Such dedication bore fruit, as the indomitable spirit of our cherished companion stirred, granting us a precious gift—additional months of shared happiness and cherished memories.

I researched what role nutrition could play in alleviating his condition and suspected that his ailment could be tied to a thyroid condition. I kept feeding him the healthiest of meals and added holistic supplements. This and Cold Laser Therapy, the same approach taken with horses, animals with long extremities like Mr. Duke.

But, life's tapestry, ever unpredictable, wove its intricate design, and fate intervened with an unforeseen turn. Consumed by a surge of emotions, I fell and fractured my wrist during an evening walk with Condesa, a beautiful rescue dog from Mexico given to me by my daughter, Gabrielle.

Mr. Duke understood the toll that had befallen me. I was scheduled for surgery one winter day in late January.

As always, Mr. Duke accompanied me to the hospital and waited for me in our SUV.

And on that cold and rainy day, as I emerged from the hospital, my body ravaged by six grueling hours of surgery, Mr. Duke chose to bid farewell to this earthly realm. He took one last look at me, and then one last breath and slept.

On that winter day, he'd taken his last trip. He'd passed away in his happiest of places, where he had traveled to discover new lands and friends, always anticipating his next adventure, his next discovery.

He took one last look
at me, and then one
last breath and slept.

So long...

He'd passed away in his favorite place, our SUV, his noble presence joining that of my dear Scooby. Their companionship, once intertwined in the realm of the living, now flourished within the embrace of eternity.
And I, with a heavy heart, believe that one day Condesa shall walk alongside them, united in joy and love.

I strongly believe that
God in his wisdom
created these
wonderful companions
to teach us humility,
unconditional love,
acceptance,
forgiveness and
all the traits that make
us better humans.

Home Meals

Wild Cod, Cauliflower and Carrots

Beef with Broccoli

Wild caught fish boiled with carrots, cauliflower, broccoli, wild mushrooms and seaweed

Grass-fed beef, chicken, broccoli, carrot, wild mushrooms and seaweed...mixed with some dry food

Holistic Approach

Understanding animal body language is important to avoid causing them unnecessary stress, especially when they are signaling a need for rest. Even my beloved Mr. Duke, who typically enjoyed long walks, sometimes showed disinterest. It's crucial not to force them to continue, as animals, like humans, can experience discomfort and anxiety.

They ask for so little yet leave behind
Thinking of you during this pai
I'm so sorry about the loss of Duke
to have such a kind and considerate fr

DUKE WILL BE MISSED.
SORRY FOR YOUR LOSS
-Justin

"May the memories of Duke bring
you comfort during this time of loss."
~ Anthony

we are gonna miss duke
was the sweetest doggo in the
wont be the same without duke
to come help us in the back, or waiting
patiently for his treats !! much love to yall!
-sophie

MOLINA FAMILY
I'm so sorry to hear about Duke, he was such a good boy, and loved his walks to the store. We're all going to miss him so much, you guys have been shopping with us from the very beginning, he was a piece of our family too.
~Robert
comfort
to know your pet
had a wonderful life
with you—
a life filled
with companionship
and love.
From your local
Pet Supplies Plus Team
We were all miss Duke very much!!
We all share in your sorrow Duke was so loved, the bond you shared can never be broken.
~Ethan
there are things only dog parents understand. I get it, and my heart aches for you. when you told me, I couldn't believe it and a held back my tears. After you left, I lost it. Duke's spirit will always be in our store and in my heart. I am going to miss Duke, too
~Nancy

Mr. Duke was happy in the city and in the trails always searching for a new adventure and winning friends

There's profound wisdom in the animal kingdom. Animal minds, like ours, resonate with emotions. Let's extend the same tenderness, love, and consideration to these fellow inhabitants of Earth, as we should to our kind.

They rely on us for their well-being. The beauty lies in their modest wants, their gentle appeals for nothing more than our care. Having grown up with various animals, I stand as a witness to their captivating allure. The bonds formed are profound, forging friendships that rival even the closest of humans.

What enchanting friendship unfolds when humans and animals bond in companionship! An inexplicable connection grows, one that transcends language. This book is a call to honor, cherish, and nurture the creatures who, in their vulnerability, seek comfort from us.

Let's exercise our authority with compassion. We should strive to comprehend their expressions. They are susceptible to both our unkindness and gentleness, and let's walk our dogs for their good and ours. It's proven that walking with your dog decreases the levels of cortisol, which is proven to reduce stress.

To my beautiful Mr. Duke, a loyal companion whose legacy pulses through these pages, I dedicate this book. His unwavering love breathed life into this book, expressing the boundless, selfless affection that only a dog can offer. You inspired this book. Rest in peace, dear Mr. Duke. Your memory dances through every word, a testimony to the profound impact of a dog's love.

You are in my heart and thoughts forever. I love you.

2010 – 2023

So long

Mr. Duke